SPECTRUM®
READERS

GREAT!
Pyramids

By Teresa Domnauer

 Carson-Dellosa
Publishing

An imprint of Carson-Dellosa Publishing, LLC
P.O. Box 35665
Greensboro, NC 27425-5665

carsondellosa.com

Printed in the USA. All rights reserved.
ISBN 978-1-4838-0118-6

01-002141120

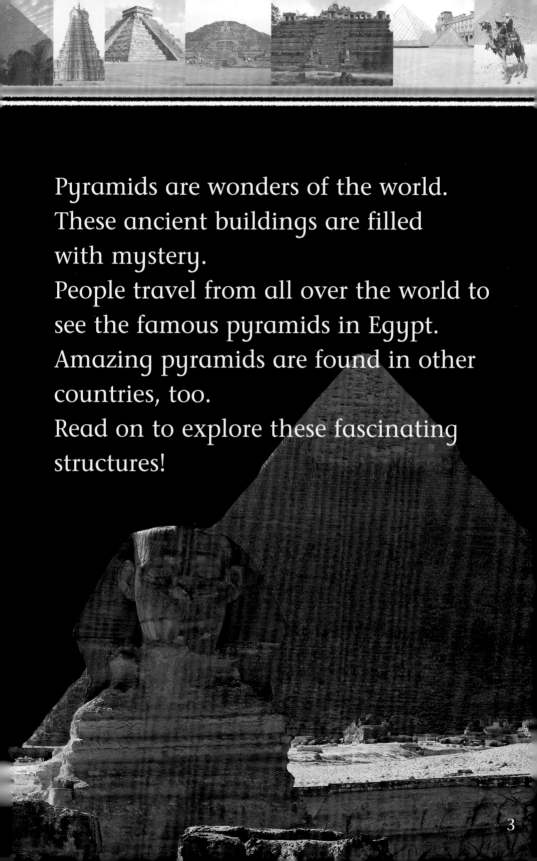

Pyramids are wonders of the world.
These ancient buildings are filled
with mystery.
People travel from all over the world to
see the famous pyramids in Egypt.
Amazing pyramids are found in other
countries, too.
Read on to explore these fascinating
structures!

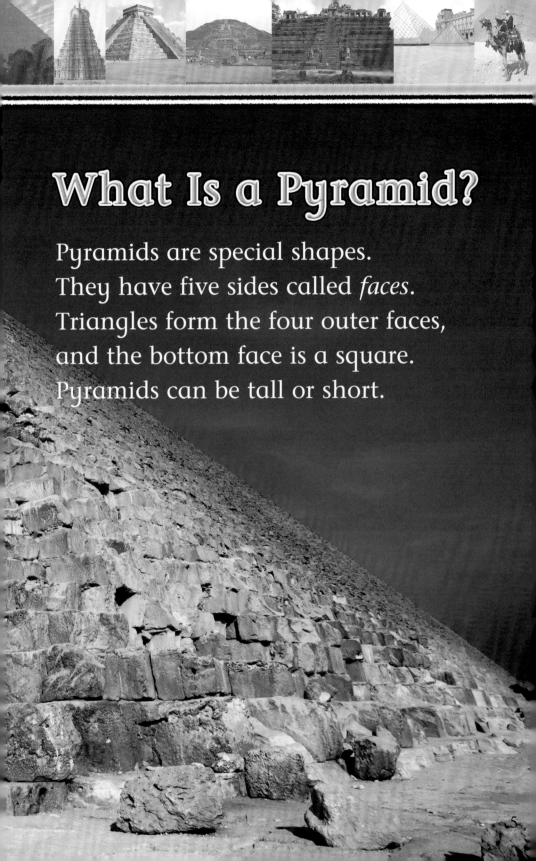

What Is a Pyramid?

Pyramids are special shapes.
They have five sides called *faces*.
Triangles form the four outer faces,
and the bottom face is a square.
Pyramids can be tall or short.

The Pyramids of Giza

Pyramids are famous.
The most well-known pyramids are the Pyramids of Giza (GHEE zah), which were built by ancient Egyptians over 4,000 years ago.
They rise from the desert outside the city of Cairo (KAI row), Egypt.

Built for Kings

Pyramids are royal.
Three ancient kings, called *pharaohs*
(FAIR ohs), ordered the Pyramids of
Giza to be built.
After they died, their mummies were
placed inside the pyramids.
The tombs were filled with statues
and other treasures.
Robbers stole most of the treasures.

Egypt's First Pyramid

Pyramids are ancient.
This pyramid was the first to be built in Egypt over 4,600 years ago. Known as a *step pyramid*, it was designed by a man named Imhotep. The step pyramid stands 204 feet high—that's as tall as a 20-story building!

Tons of Stone

Pyramids are stone.
To build them, workers lifted thousands
of limestone blocks for many years.
Each block weighed as much as a car,
and workers did not have machines to
help them.
Experts still cannot explain exactly
how the pyramids were built.

The Great Pyramid

Pyramids are massive.
The largest pyramid on Earth is the
Great Pyramid of Giza.
Made from over two million stone
blocks, it was built for a pharaoh
named Khufu (KOO foo).
It stands 451 feet high, as tall as a
small mountain.
Many passageways and rooms hide
below this enormous pyramid.

Guarding the Pyramids

Pyramids are protected.

A giant stone sculpture, the Great Sphinx (SFINKS), stands near the Pyramids of Giza.

It has a man's face and a lion's body. People believe the Great Sphinx guards the Great Pyramid.

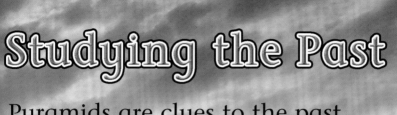

Studying the Past

Pyramids are clues to the past.
Archaeologists study pyramids to learn
how people lived thousands of years ago.
They read picture writing, called
hieroglyphics, on pyramid walls.
They dig for things left behind by
thousands of workers who lived nearby.

A Pyramid in India

Pyramids are works of art.
Decorative carvings cover this
nine-level temple in India.
Stones that look like cow horns jut out
from the top.
Festivals with parades, elephants, and
dancers happen here every year.

Pyramids in Mexico

Pyramids are calendars.
This flat-topped pyramid in Mexico has 365 steps, one for each day of the year.
On two special days each year, shadows cast by the setting sun look like a snake wriggling down the steps!

Pyramid of the Sun

Pyramids are sturdy.
This pyramid in Mexico was once
part of a large city.
The city is gone, but the Pyramid of
the Sun still stands after 2,000 years.
Archaeologists are not sure which
ancient people built it so well.

A Pyramid in Cambodia

Pyramids are legendary.
This temple in the forests of Cambodia
was built over 1,000 years ago.
Ancient bathing pools surround it.
Legend says that a nine-headed snake
lived inside.

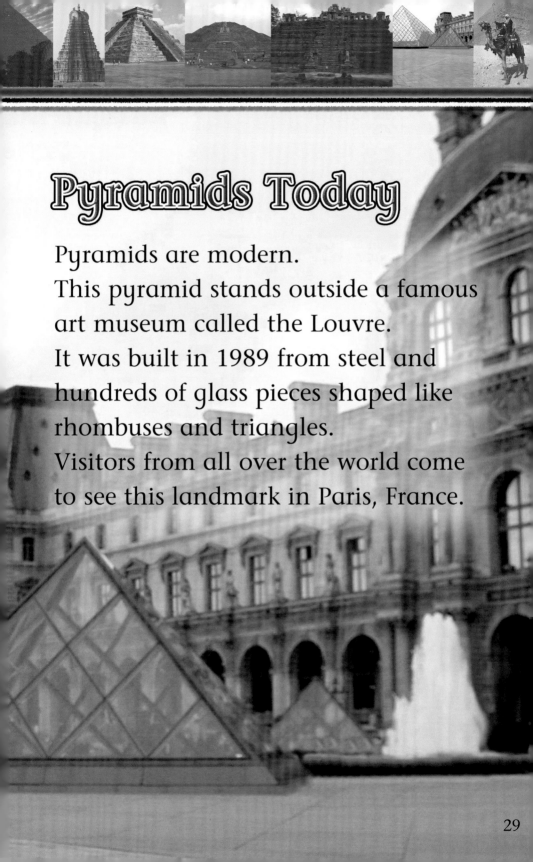

Pyramids Today

Pyramids are modern.
This pyramid stands outside a famous art museum called the Louvre.
It was built in 1989 from steel and hundreds of glass pieces shaped like rhombuses and triangles.
Visitors from all over the world come to see this landmark in Paris, France.

Still Fascinating

Pyramids are fascinating.
People have been attracted to them
for thousands of years.
Archaeologists continue to study them.
People travel far and wide to see them.
They are an amazing and mysterious
part of the world's history.

GREAT! Pyramids
Comprehension Questions

1. What shapes make up the five faces of a pyramid?

2. What kind of stone are the Egyptian pyramids made of?

3. What does the body of the Great Sphinx look like?

4. Why do archaeologists study pyramids?

5. What happened to many treasures inside the Pyramids of Giza?

6. What is an Egyptian king called?

7. Name three places in the world where pyramids can be found.

8. When does the light on a Mexican pyramid look like a snake?

9. What materials were used to build a modern pyramid in France?